"Writing from a global p invite us to understand biblical and interdependent [...] across financial and cultural divides. This is must reading for any North American desiring to serve alongside the church of the Majority World."

Paul Borthwick, author of *Western Christians in Global Mission* and *How to Be a World-Class Christian*

"In this significant contribution to the urgent and unfolding global conversation on missional partnership, Femi Adeleye and Nikki Toyama-Szeto illuminate the whys of partnership—an essential component in bearing witness to hope. As globalization makes the world more accessible and smaller than ever, Femi and Nikki offer a clear road map to partnership based on interdependency. With thoughtful sensitivity and courage, tackling some of the most difficult issues in crosscultural partnerships, Femi and Nikki navigate the nuanced challenges of negotiating the complex power dynamics in missional partnerships. Affirming the preeminence of God already at work in the world, *Partnering with the Global Church* approaches this delicate conversation with humility, while maintaining confidence and conviction."

Christopher L. Heuertz, senior strategist, Word Made Flesh, author of *Unexpected Gifts* and *Simple Spirituality*

"As the authors note, 'Partnership is not an option—it is an essential.' This much-needed publication will be helpful both to those who think otherwise and those who haven't given partnership much thought. God's intention for partnerships is often misunderstood, and the authors redirect via Scripture and their thoughtful reflection and instruction, as well as Spirit-led experiences for immediate application. Recommended reading for anyone serving God's kingdom, from collegians to Christian leaders; required reading for every missionary."

Rev. Melanie Mar Chow, campus minister with Asian American Christian Fellowship/JEMS

.

URBANA ONWARD

Partnering with the Global Church

NIKKI A. TOYAMA-SZETO
AND FEMI B. ADELEYE

Series editors:
Nikki A. Toyama-Szeto and Tom Lin

≈≈
IVP Books

An imprint of InterVarsity Press
Downers Grove, Illinois

InterVarsity Press
P.O. Box 1400, Downers Grove, IL 60515-1426
World Wide Web: www.ivpress.com
E-mail: email@ivpress.com

InterVarsity Press® is the book-publishing division of InterVarsity Christian Fellowship/USA®, a movement of students and faculty active on campus at hundreds of universities, colleges and schools of nursing in the United States of America, and a member movement of the International Fellowship of Evangelical Students. For information about local and regional activities, write Public Relations Dept., InterVarsity Christian Fellowship/USA, 6400 Schroeder Rd., P.O. Box 7895, Madison, WI 53707-7895, or visit the IVCF website at <www.intervarsity.org>.

All Scripture quotations, unless otherwise indicated, are taken from the Holy Bible, Today's New International Version®, NIV® Copyright © 1973, 1978, 1984, 2011 by Biblica, Inc.™ Used by permission. All rights reserved worldwide.

While all stories in this book are true, some names and identifying information in this book have been changed to protect the privacy of the individuals involved.

Cover design: Cindy Kiple
Images: abstract background: © Matthew Hertel/iStockphoto
        gear: © Matthew Hertel/iStockphoto
ISBN 978-0-8308-3460-0

Printed in the United States of America ∞

green press INITIATIVE   InterVarsity Press is committed to protecting the environment and to the responsible use of natural resources. As a member of Green Press Initiative we use recycled paper whenever possible. To learn more about the Green Press Initiative, visit <www .greenpressinitiative.org>.

Library of Congress Cataloging-in-Publication Data has been requested.

P	21	20	19	18	17	16	15	14	13	12	11	10	9	8	7	6	5	4	3	2	1
Y	30	29	28	27	26	25	24	23	22	21	20	19	18	17	16	15	14	13	12

Contents

The body of Christ is as dynamic as it is alive in most contexts of the world. It is as vibrant as it is contemplative and as resilient in silence as it is outspoken. God in his wisdom and generosity has not entrusted all the riches of Christ to any one particular culture—lest anyone should boast. Rather he has impacted all nations with the grace of our Lord Jesus Christ and the outcome is what we see expressed in different contexts. How then should we benefit from this and maximize the impact of these riches of grace for the advancement of the kingdom? Even if the word has been overused, the best way is through *partnership*. Not just partnership in ministry or mission, but partnership in fellowship.

PROBLEMS WITH PARTNERSHIP

Partnership is a common word, but remains an elusive practice. When practiced well, all parties involved find themselves making meaningful and significant contributions, and the mission is undeniably moved forward. It is African church pastors bringing vibrancy to a spiritually latent London neighborhood church. The combination of prophetic faith brought by these missional pastors and the relational invitations of local members mixes to create a vibrant faith community. But practiced poorly, the result might be ineffectiveness, broken relationships and short-lived vision. A local large church and smaller church decided to merge—the larger church had people, money and resources; the struggling church had a strategic location and buildings. But in the process, the larger church made assumptions that their money dictated the direction, and they acted in a way that alienated the smaller church and a mutually beneficial union became a dysfunctional mess.

Both of us have experienced partnerships in a variety of contexts. As a Nigerian who worked in the United States, Europe and Africa, Femi brings a unique perspective. He brings observations from his work as the associate general secretary of partnership and collaboration for the International Fellowship of Evangelical Students—IFES is a partnership of student movements in about 145 countries. In his current role he works crossculturally with IFES member movements worldwide to nurture and enable partnerships within the global fellowship. He also works to build bridges for mutually beneficial collaboration between IFES and churches, as well as like-minded organizations such as the Langham Partnership, the Lausanne Movement and the Global Christian Forum.

Nikki works as an Asian American woman building partnerships with individuals, churches and organizations in the United States. She directs the development of the Urbana Student Missions Conference in partnership with various groups—church leaders, campus ministry workers, missiologists and artists. She researches and observes various groups and missions movements trying to understand best practices and trends. She has served in various national boards and international settings, including the Lausanne Movement.

"I can tell you what partnership is not," said Antonio to Nikki on a recent visit to Latin America. "A group comes down to visit us. We take them into a favela, they take pictures of the kids and use it to raise money that we never see."

Another chimed in, "Sometimes groups come down with a project that they've created, and then just do it. They don't ask us."

A hospital in Kenya received the gift of a new, state-of-the-art hospital. But because of the lack of partnership, this modern hospital was rendered useless. The designers, donors and organization never talked with the people who would use or run the hospital. So while there was a heart and coronary section comparable to the best found in Western hospitals, the doctors were unable to do any procedures because they didn't have paper to document basic medical records. The modern equipment for x-rays stayed unused because there wasn't film for the x-rays or even basic medicines to treat wounds. Items found in a first-aid kit in the United States were not available, though there were stations to prep for complicated surgeries. The lack of local partnership resulted in good intentions becoming a waste of resources.

Partnership is often misconceived in two ways. One is the idea of partnership as exchanging resources such as funds or skills. The other is going into other people's communities to do projects. As good as these may be as aspects of partnership, they may become the primary motivation, and the very essence of partnership is lost. We make the mistake of equating partnership with going into other people's context with skills and resources, and doing projects. That in itself can become an obstacle to what God is already doing or how he wants to work in any given context.

Some use *partnership* as a code word for "money" or "splitting the cost between two groups of people." "I can't afford to do this great idea, but that group has a lot of money—let's invite them to be 'partners.'" My idea, their money. Is this partnership?

But partnership that God calls us to is so different from these previous examples. We take our very cues from God himself, who could accomplish everything on his own but gives us the privilege of being included in his work. Partnership, as provided by God, is an opportunity to pursue his purposes as a family of God. It's a chance to recognize the great ways God is working through others nearby, and to work in complement with them. It purifies our motives, our methods and our very selves as we pursue God's purposes.

Being with must precede any *doing*. It is in being together that we begin to understand what God is already doing with people in any given place. Our primary goal must not be to go and provide resources or do things for other people. It should be to strengthen relationships by being with and becoming part of what God wants to do with us together in any given context. God is already at work in every cultural context, including "unreached people" or "access restricted" contexts. That understanding should free us of any misplaced concept of being messianic interventionists.

ONE BODY, MANY PARTS

Partnership begins when we realize that we are all part of one body. In 1 Corinthians 12:12-26 Paul paints a picture of what partnership or fellowship in Christ looks like. It's a picture of various parts of the body working together and functioning in unity.

Paul writes that while the body is one, it is made of many parts. It is the baptism in the same Spirit that gives us unity despite the distinctions the world places on each of the parts (v. 13).

Paul makes the case that all parts belong to the same body. The foot says that because it is not a hand it does not belong (v. 15). But these distinctions do not give any part an excuse to not be a part of the body. He says that a body full of all the same parts would miss out on other essential functions. God placed each part in the body where he wanted each to be (v. 18).

In the one body certain parts do not despise other parts and decide to live separate from the body (v. 21). Paul addresses the possible distinctions that may exacerbate division and discord. He states that the perceived "weaker" parts are essential to the body (v. 22). The parts that are considered less honorable are treated with special honor. And the unpresentable parts

---

One Body, Many Parts

(1 Corinthians 12)

- *Each is part of the body (vv. 15-17).*

- *No part should disdain its role; God placed each in its place (v. 18).*

- *Each part is needed—no part can say, "I don't need you" (v. 21).*

- *Do not be divided.*
  - *Parts that seem weaker are essential (v. 22).*
  - *Treat parts that are less regarded with more honor (v. 23).*
  - *Treat unpresentable parts with special modesty (v. 23).*
  - *Special treatment is not needed for the presentable parts (v. 24).*

- *Have equal concern for each other—suffer together, rejoice together (vv. 25-26).*

are treated with modesty (v. 23). The presentable parts need no special treatment (v. 24). God has put together the body, and it—the one body—has one purpose.

Paul's final exhortation calls all the parts to participate in the suffering of the one part to rejoice in the honor of another (v. 26).

This picture challenges us to ask whether we have assumed that we were "doing" things for our potential partners. Is the foot trying to solve a problem for the hand? We need to reorient our thinking to one-body living: how can the hand and the foot work well together? How can we live out being a part of one body?

WHY DO PARTNERSHIP?

I (Nikki) worked for John Deere, a major American manufacturer of agricultural and construction equipment. I noticed an intriguing dynamic. This company made large machines for both construction and agriculture. In a discussion with both departments I noticed a switch. In the agricultural field, this company was number one. As they talked about other companies, there was no need or interest in working with them. But in the construction area, this company was third or fourth in the field. As they talked about their competition, there was a lot of interest in "partnerships" and "working together" so they could "collaborate." It was striking to me that where they were strong they were not interested in working with others and in effect sharing that expertise. But in the areas where they knew they needed help, they were very interested in partnering.

Could this same dynamic be happening with North Americans as we think about partnership? If we feel we have the answers, perhaps we also feel that there is no need to include others to proceed. If we can buy our own supplies, make our own arrangements, we feel that we don't need and don't involve others. Is it only when we feel we need help that we think about partnership? Or perhaps we disqualify people as potential partners because we don't think they have something to add.

By A.D. 600 Christianity had spread to North Africa and southern Europe. The heart of Christendom was largely Rome and Constantinople. Yet the gospel was not meant for the Mediterranean world alone. After another dispersal from a place of comfort (and theological debates), as well as the difficult challenge of the rise of Islam, Christianity declined in North Africa and the Middle East, and spread throughout Europe by A.D. 1000. With various revivals in England, Wales, Germany and so forth, Europe then became the cradle of Christianity. The gospel was also not meant for Europe alone. Hence there was a further dispersal from the comfort zone of civilized exclusiveness. The spread of Christianity to North America was marked by Great Awakenings and social impact that largely redefined Christianity as a predominantly Western faith or religion. But God was not finished yet. The gospel was not meant for the West alone. It had to move on to the ends of the Earth.

Recent developments in missions trends and Christian history have confirmed time and again what Andrew Walls has described as "the passing of the Christian centre of gravity from the west to the south."[1] By the south, Walls means the non-Western world. Patrick Johnstone calls this the "globalization of Christianity."[2] This shift in the Christian center of gravity has been marked by the rapid growth and expansion of Christianity in non-Western contexts that used to be predominantly non-Christian. There is also a generation of missionaries moving, not from the West to other parts of the world but from the non-Western world into territories that were once regarded as the Christian world. In 1900 it was estimated that 88 percent of the world's Christians lived in Europe and North America. In 1992, according to the *World Christian Encyclopedia* an estimate of 60 percent of the world's Christians lived in Africa, Asia and Latin America.[3]

Andrew Walls prophetically declared that there has been "a demographic shift in the centre of gravity of the Christian world, which means that more than half of the world's Christians live in Africa, Asia, Latin America, or the Pacific, and that the proportion doing so grows annually." Walls goes as far as saying that "the Christianity typical of the twenty-first century will be shaped by events and processes that take place in the southern continents, and above all by those that take place in Africa."[4]

Furthermore, the rapidly emerging church is not waiting for the gospel to be preached in the same way it was a hundred years ago.

Whereas the primary focus then was to get people saved and prepared for heaven, the church in the Majority World is grappling with how kingdom values can be brought to bear on contemporary issues, such as rampant corruption in spite of rapid church growth, good and bad governance, HIV/AIDS, and others too many to be mentioned. This generation of missionaries must be equipped to deal with some of these pressing challenges.

We must think through ways of meaningful engagement with these realities. And robust partnerships help us engage deeply with the complexity of these issues and the depth of God's love.

Some of these observations raise uneasy questions. Some have suggested that, with the emergence of the church in the Global South, the era of Western nations sending missionaries is over. Again Paul reminds us that the body does not consist of just one member but many. If the ear would say, "Because I am not an eye, I do not belong to the body," that would not make it any less a part of the body (1 Corinthians 12:16). The work of God's mission does not belong solely to the church of the Global South, in the same way that it was never the domain of the Western church.

Only the Lord of the harvest can call a halt to missionary movements, and there is no indication that he has. What is more obvious today is that mission has now become from anywhere to everywhere, and we must all participate! Gospel choirs from America have profound ministry in Japan. Brazilian missionaries head to Italy to reignite Christian communities. Indigenous people journey to the Holy Land, taking the gospel from the "ends of the earth" back to Israel in a fantastic reversal of Acts 1:8. Korean missionaries carry the gospel to Mongolia and ethnic minority groups in China. Nigerian missionaries establish communities in London and American cities.

Crosscultural partnership needs to bear in mind and celebrate the diversity of today's global church. The church is multinational, multicultural, multiethnic, multicolored and multigifted! Worship and service ascend to the throne of God with diverse gifts from the ends of the earth to demonstrate the manifold wisdom of God! From Boston to Botswana, from Beijing to Berlin, from Jerusalem to Johannesburg, from New York to New

Delhi and from Morocco to Monaco, the rich diversity of the church empowers us for greater witness. We have such a rich heritage in the adventurous spirit of early missionaries from North America and Europe, in the perseverance and suffering of Eastern block missionaries, and in the pain and suffering of diverse martyrs of the faith. Consider the beauty of the buoyant and celebrative life of the Latin American church. The contemplative retreat of those in the monastic tradition across the world and the pure delight of worship among Ethiopian students are treasures for the global church. Who can forget the sobriety and anticipation of Korean or Malaysian Christians in prayer? The resilience and perseverance of those under affliction in various parts of the world fuel larger pictures of God's faithfulness. The African sense of transcendence and the engaging interaction between the natural and supernatural world are reminders of God's involvement in the routines of our daily life.

Today, partly as a result of both Western and non-Western missionary endeavors, the passion of recipient nations and, more significantly, God's sovereign grace, there is a rapidly emerging church in various parts of the world. There has been significant church growth in the least expected places. Who could have imagined that there would be any good news from the churches in Khartoum? In the face of government repression and severe persecution, more than two thousand students attend mission conferences regularly in Khartoum. Students in Khartoum once told me, "The Muslim world sees Khartoum as the gateway for Islam to penetrate the rest of Africa, *but* we see Khartoum as the gateway for the gospel to penetrate all of North Africa and the Middle East." Those young people are the pioneers of church planting and renewal in the new nation of South Sudan! At one time, we might have scoffed at the idea of a place like Khartoum as a potential partner.

These are essential realities for crosscultural mission partners to bear in mind. We must stop thinking of crosscultural missions in the sense of those going from the West to the Global South. We need the eternal perspective to appreciate the significance of what is going on here! The transmission of the gospel through diverse cultures contributes to God's beautiful mosaic of what the church should be as it journeys toward the final banquet when every nation and tongue will bow in worship before the Lamb of God on the throne. As John records,

> After this I looked, and there before me was a great multitude that no one could count, from every nation, tribe, people and language, standing before the throne and before the Lamb. They were wearing white robes and were holding palm branches in their hands. And they cried out in a loud voice:
>
> "Salvation belongs to our God,
> who sits on the throne,
> and to the Lamb." (Revelation 7:9-10)

To be honest, sometimes I (Nikki) think that I'm right. I trust my gut. I have good intuition and I'm smart. Working with other people slows me down. And sometimes I find myself having to fight for the things that I am very interested in. It's easier to do it myself. And I don't have to compromise. But I have blind spots. I only have *my* experiences to draw from. And I only have *my* perspective to analyze information. Until I have a healthy skepticism of myself, I will probably not look for partnerships. And global trends tell me that North Americans should have a healthy skepticism when it comes to the growth of the church.

But a particular experience shaped me for life. During leadership training, my church group was led through a group exercise called the NASA moon-landing exercise.[5] Basically, each person is given a list of items that he or she is to put in order of usefulness in an emergency during a moon landing. Based on information from a NASA exercise, the question is asked, What do you need to reach the rendezvous point? The exercise measures your ability to think in different contexts. Feeling pretty confident, I set about ranking my list. I was pretty sure I would have one of the highest scores. I had studied to be a mechanical engineer with the hope of becoming an astronaut. We were then instructed to form groups of two to five people and come up with a group list. After that was finished, we scored our list against the NASA official list.

Expecting to be the winning group, we started to compare the group scores to the individual scores. In every team the group scored better than any individual! I was shocked—and humbled. I was sure that my perspective would be better—I was, after all, a graduate of Space Academy (I and II)! The exercise tests what it calls "gravity-based thinking." Two one-hundred-pound tanks of oxygen are the top item on the NASA list. But the weight (or size) of the tanks put me off. Weight and bulk are not an issue in space the way that they are on earth. My number seven item, matches, is listed as the last item on the NASA list—matches are virtually useless in space even though they are so essential on Earth. The assumptions we make are based on our earthbound experiences—but have no relevancy in space. So working in groups, people tend to uncover more of their assumptions, more of their blind spots about life in space. This lesson has influenced my work since.

We all have limitations or "gravity-based assumptions" that we might not even realize. For example, a small company tries to do justice with its product, but its production line doesn't fulfill fair labor requirements. A ministry set to reach out to youth in an urban area designs a program that doesn't accommodate the work schedule of students in the neighborhood. The intentions are good, but without local partnerships good intentions can result in ineffective programs.

Christian partnership proclaims "there are some things you know about God that I don't." Paul points out the tendency for believers to think that we're sufficient in and of ourselves. "If the whole body were an eye, where would the sense of hearing be?" (1 Corinthians 12:17). The reality is that we are all baptized into one body. Some parts of the body are hands—and they know well how to reach out and pick up something. But others are the liver, and they know how to clean the blood, which provides resources for muscles, which help the hand to pick items up. Similarly, some of us know or experience God in ways that others don't. We need to work as members of a whole body, rather than as individual specialized parts. "The eye cannot say to the hand, 'I don't need of you!'" (1 Corinthians 12:21).

Global partnership fills out and expands our picture of God.

PARTNERSHIP TAKES PRACTICE

In view of this, what should crosscultural partnership be? The starting point is being with one another to know each other well enough to be able to serve together. As we do this we'll increasingly discover that the ground is equal at the foot of the cross of Christ. In true mission partnership no participant is superior or inferior to the other. We must appreciate that all have something to offer, and that the gifting and resources applied to partnership ultimately belongs to God and not to us.

Having established this, partnership must involve listening to and learning from all that God is doing globally, identifying situations of needs and of resources in God's world and working with likeminded people to effectively match resources with needs for maximum kingdom impact. The listening and learning process must be mutual. In other words it is not only those in need who must listen and learn. Well-resourced people and organizations must also listen and learn. It is in the listening process that we together learn values, community and dependence on God. Resources are not just monetary or financial. They include prayer, fellowship, skills and expertise—as well as the material or financial. Beyond listening, learning and sharing with one another, true partnership advances the cause of the gospel and affects God's world with compassion. We must practice listening and learning from others, as well as sharing.

In other parts of the world, partnership is not an option—it is essential. But in North America we can be blinded by our access to resources, believing that we don't need others. Missionaries from the Latin American context do not have the same luxuries that North Americans do. Their passports do not get them quite so far. Their money doesn't provide all that they need. So there is an inherent reality of interdependency.

Latinos are some of the most effective missionaries to the Middle East. I (Nikki) met missionaries from the Dominican Republic who were planning their third and fourth short-term trips to various Middle Eastern countries. American missionaries have a tough time doing ministry in the Middle East. Tensions and political issues between the United States and leaders in the region precede and affect the perceptions Middle Easterners have of Americans. But I was struck by the work of missionaries from the Dominican Republic. They don't have the American tourist dollar behind them granting a visa and allowing them to go in uninvited. These Dominican missionaries need to secure an invitation and a local place to stay. They have to know who else is in the town, because they don't have the money to rent a building or pay for a hotel room. Before they arrive, they have to secure housing, an invitation and other items that North Americans acquire through a credit card. They don't have the luxuries and access that comes with being an American. But because of their need, they are in some ways better prepared to be salt and light in that community.

Practice interdependency. When tempted to take care of your needs yourself through finances, your own networks or utilizing your own gifts, consider ways you can involve others and practice the fellowship of the body. Instead of finding a hotel room in a new place, discover how people in the community you're partnering with handle housing. Is it common for people to stay in someone's house? Interdependency requires vulnerable action and choice. But the eye cannot tell the hand, "I have no need of you."

In Luke 10 Jesus sends the seventy-two out in mission. He commanded them not to take a purse, a bag or sandals (v. 4), challenging them to rely on his provision in the context of pursing the mission. What does it mean to let go of our temptation to be self-reliant and instead practice living as part of the body, interdependently with other parts?

When I (Nikki) was team leader at University of California, Berkeley, every year we received one or two groups that wanted to plant a Christian fellowship on campus. I believe they thought that Berkeley was a pagan wasteland. I'm not sure what gave them that idea—was it the naked people walking around on campus, the liberal reputation, the debauchery that poured out onto Telegraph Avenue from very sketchy cafes?

So every year I would receive calls from someone sent from a church or organization to start a ministry on campus. But despite the appearance of a pagan wasteland—here's the reality. UC Berkeley has one of the most vibrant Christian communities I've seen. There are seventy Christian groups registered on campus. At a recent Urbana Student Missions Conference, UC Berkeley had the largest campus representation. One out of every one hundred people at Urbana was a Berkeley student. The Christians who graduate from Berkeley are world Christians—they have a vision as big as the world. I think that's why there's so much "crazy." The enemy is trying to stir up trouble because God is doing so much good on that campus.

So when someone told me they wanted to start a new fellowship at Berkeley, I must admit, it was hard. Because the reality was that California State University, East Bay, a campus about twenty minutes away, had only two Christian groups. I longed to see that campus also reached, even though it did not have the glossy reputation of Berkeley. The intentions of these various ministries were good—I was glad that they had a heart for UC Berkeley. But I wondered if they had a heart for a pagan wasteland campus that mostly existed in their minds, but not based on reality.

On the UC Berkeley campus, we received well-meaning church revivals and evangelism blitzes. Some groups started and thrived, others failed. Some groups helped; other groups made our work and relationships more strained.

Practice assuming God is already at work. God is the originator of mission, and he's the one who invited you in. Instead of assuming you are the only missionary or Christian worker with a heart for a place, practice good partnership: look to see who is doing a similar work, learn from others, come alongside them. See if God has prepared partners for you already. If no one is there, ask around to find out about the history of the place. Talk to churches or other faith communities in the area. Assess the spiritual climate of a place.

Crosscultural partners must bear in mind that it is a different church out there! The world is no longer the unreached "pagan" world it was one hundred or so years ago. The early disciples and apostles were very passionate and irrepressible in the obedience of Jesus' command to be witnesses to him "in Jerusalem, and in all Judea and Samaria, and to the ends of the earth" (Acts 1:8). Christianity began with a handful of disciples as a Jewish church. However the gospel was not meant for the nation of

Israel alone. If the church had remained Jewish, it would be less than God intends it to be. Gentiles also needed to become part of God's family. Hence God moved the early church out of the comfort zone of its Jewish culture, expanding it to include Gentiles, mostly in the Middle East and western Asia. Even then the gospel was not meant for Asia Minor alone. While the church had its roots in Jerusalem, crosscultural mission began in an organized way from Antioch. Jesus had given the command to go to the ends of the earth. In obedience to the command of Jesus the church in Antioch sent out Paul and Barnabas.

Our world is perplexing and its perception is sometimes clouded by the impact of Western nations in economic and military matters, including the sanctions they have imposed on a number of nations. Do these issues have anything to do with how we do mission or partner? Certainly so!

I (Femi), writing to you as a member of the body, can say the world was very angry at the Western invasion of Iraq and is still angry at the imposition of American and Western (to a large extent Hollywood) values on traditional cultures of non-Western nations. Yes, Western Christians are not necessarily responsible for most of these, but the consequences have implications for every partner. According to Meic Pearse, non-Westerners are understandably anxious about the future of their cultural space, which they feel is threatened by aliens—that is, by the West.[6] "And to the non-West, our culture [i.e., Western culture] appears not as a culture at all, but as an anticulture. Our values appear not as an alternative to traditional values but as a negation of them—as anti-values, in fact."[7] Earlier, in the introduction of his book, he says, "For most of the nineteenth and twentieth centuries, Westerners hardly felt they need to take alternative world views seriously, since Western values, customs, and ideas seemed obviously set to dominate the world."[8]

But as events around the world have shown, and as Meic Pearse affirms in his book, most parts of the non-Western world are resistant to the imposition of Western influences. "The great civilizations of Asia—Chinese, Hindu, Japanese and others—are declining the offer of further assimilation along Western lines."[9] And I will add that most parts of Africa would only concede to these influences as long as their cultural roots and values are not violated. In view of this, Meic concludes that "Westerners can no longer act on the bland assumption that their ideas about what constitutes common sense are universal or beyond examination."[10]

Practice identification with others in their world and realities. It is key that Jesus-followers understand this. The world not only needs to be understood by those who will be involved out there, but counter-culture missionaries are needed. People who have deliberately emptied themselves of popular assumptions of Western culture and whose lifestyles point to Christ and not their own. On issues of international injustice, I (Femi) believe God also needs missionaries out there, not working in traditional Christian institutions but within international organizations like the United Nations to infiltrate them with the justice and righteousness of a global God. The practice of living counterculturally is also a practice of identifying with our global body.

Good partnership requires a certain level of humility—an acknowledgment that "this will be better if more people are involved than just myself." But Christian partnership takes this a step further—it's an acknowledgment that God's purposes

Partnership Practices

- *Practice listening and learning.*

- *Practice interdependency.*

- *Practice assuming God is already at work.*

- *Practice giving and receiving from others, learning and teaching.*

- *Practice identification with others in their world and realities.*

- *Practice paying attention to the effects of power on communication, decisions and resources.*

- *Cultivate the practices of being a partner in yourself, your group, your organization before entering into a partnership.*

need all types of people to be accomplished. His ways are not clouded by prejudice, cultural perspectives or past experiences. God's ways require many people, each contributing their specialized role, all working together and in fellowship to make up the whole body.

Before Philip got to the Ethiopian eunuch on the way to Gaza, God was already at work with him (Acts 8:26-40). And before Peter got to Cornelius in Caesarea, God was already at work in his household and community (Acts 10). In both cases the partners came only to participate in what God was already doing as his mission. Likewise when early missionaries came to Africa, they did not bring God or Christ to us. God was already present and at work with us in diverse ways. Quite often even pagan priests foretold the coming of mission partners. Such revelation was not just human. It is therefore critical as we consider partnership to bear in mind that we do not initiate mission. God does! The greatest skills we need to foster lasting partnership are a sensitive listening ear and the discernment of what God is already doing in any given context. Our involvement is often partaking in a meal that God was cooking before we got there.

SOME PRACTICAL STEPS TOWARD BECOMING A BETTER PARTNER

- Do some research. Who else cares about this? Has someone else worked on this before, with this group of people? Is there someone/a church in the community I should talk to in order to learn more?

- If your project idea is supposed to help a group of people, considering inviting someone from the "target" group to be a part of designing the solution.

- Spend some time with prospective partners—get to know them, their context, their values, their worldview.

- Be curious, ask questions, and keep a learning posture.

POWER UNDERMINES PARTNERSHIP

One of the downfalls of a promising partnership is neglecting to pay attention to power. In many interactions there are those who have more power and others who have less. And when people are working to form a partnership, it's very important to pay attention to how power affects communication, decision making, resources and conflicts.

Power is often invisible to those who have it, and visible to those who don't. As North Americans entering into partnerships with those in the Majority World, we may have more power than we realize. Power may be expressed by our gender, education, socioeconomic status, geography, education level.

For example, power becomes visible when we look at the experience of two different people (with different levels of power) at a hotel front desk. Two people could have similar interactions but a totally different experience. And they would each come away with different conclusions about that hotel.

A guest at a hotel (access is a form of power) will come up to the desk and ask for directions to go to the pool. When the guest flashes her room key, the front desk person is very helpful: "Go up the stairs, to the right and put your key in the slot. Have a great day."

But someone else who doesn't have a hotel room could ask the same question. When asked for a room key, he doesn't show it. He doesn't have one. He insists on directions to the pool, but the front desk is not welcoming and resists providing directions. This person complains that the front desk was rude and not helpful.

When talking with the second person, the first person could come to the conclusion that he is just a complainer—the front desk is quite nice. But what she doesn't realize is that it wasn't just a personal interaction. She had privileges, stemming from her position of power as a guest at the hotel, that influenced the interaction with the person at the front desk. She benefitted from the invisible privilege that power provides.

In some situations we are the people with power. Other times, we are the people without much power. Whether it's our race, nationality, gender, experience, age, income level, the language we speak or personality, different attributes in different contexts give power to some while withholding it from others. Pretending no one has power may seem like a good idea, but it is actually disingenuous. If we do not acknowledge that there are power differences, it is impossible to address them. These seemingly insignificant elements will slowly undermine good partnership.

Paul understood this dynamic as he said that honor and special consideration is given to those body parts that need it so that we might be unified. Unacknowledged power has a way of eroding good partnerships.

Paying attention to how power affects our communication, our decisions and our priorities will help us to be better partners. Good intentions and the misuse of power can lead to accidental exploitation. But good intentions and the mindful stewardship of power can lead to empowering relationships.

PRACTICING PARTNERSHIP, BEFORE IT HAPPENS

Practice being a good partner where you already are. Many people want to jump into partnership, but there are many half-steps they can take that would actually help them to be better partners. And there are lots of ways to practice, make mistakes and learn to become a great partner without putting partnerships at risk.

Practicing the skills of partnership is possible on every level. In your fellowship or church, is there a group that is on the margin? What does it mean to be a better partner to those who are already in your midst? For example, right-handed people and left-handed people? Men and women? What can you learn about different ways of doing life that make your group more accessible to those who are already part of it but on the edges? Maybe your group accidentally sets up its tables in ways that make it particularly uncomfortable for left-handed people! Doing well with the microcultures in our groups is a great way to prepare for bigger partnerships.

Or perhaps your group excludes certain socioeconomic groups. I was part of a church that often went out to eat for lunch after the worship service. Those who could afford to go to a restaurant every week would probably think, *What a friendly church*, but those who couldn't would comment that it's hard to get to know people. Are there ways your group functions that isolates or alienates others? What does it mean to redefine how you relate and practice partnership?

Perhaps you're interested in setting up a partnership with another group internationally. Instead of going to their place first, consider inviting them to your context first, showing them around and asking them to reflect to you what they see. And at their invitation, ask if there's anything they see that would be helpful to bring to their context.

If you're part of an organization wanting to have more global partnership, how racially diverse is your organization? Try working on that first and becoming a culturally and racially diverse organization before trying to be global. For example, multiethnic issues have very similar dynamics to crosscultural issues. The skills are transferable. But the nice thing about working with other, diverse North Americans is they can tell you what is challenging about your organization's culture in a way that might be very difficult for Majority World leaders to do (since there are so many other dynamics like money, power and communication styles).

FRUITS OF PARTNERSHIP

In the early 2000s, my (Nikki's) Christian fellowship, which was one of the largest and oldest student organizations on the campus, decided to focus some attention on Darfur. We felt convicted to call attention to the atrocities happening there. We could have caused a stir ourselves, but we realized there were others who probably knew more about the situation. As well, there might be other groups on campus that were already working on this. We set out to find out.

In the process we worked with the Hillel group—a Jewish campus group of about ten people. They were also interested and already working to raise campus awareness. So together we started the Students Taking Action Now for Darfur (STAND)—InterVarsity and Hillel. Our group brought about three hundred folks to the conversation.

We could have done it alone. But it ended being a great experience. We built new relationships and had intense spiritual conversations with our new partners. The excitement and enthusiasm was huge. We had people power. They had a transformative experience. They discovered that Christians were interested in this great injustice. It reordered their assumptions about Christians. They taught our group about the issues and complexities at play. Our group learned how to turn good intentions into motivation to get educated. We also were held accountable to not use the justice cause as an evangelism tool. It would be an accidental form of exploitation of the people of Darfur.

It is important for crosscultural mission partners to bear in mind that the emerging church in various parts of the world has a mind of its own as it reflects on biblical truth. Not only that, it wants to be taken seriously. In the past there was open embrace and acceptance of almost everything Western missionaries introduced or nurtured. We now have a church that draws a line between the essence of the gospel and Western culture. The growing non-Western church is increasingly growing out of being on the receiving end and moving into greater partnership/participation in *missio Dei.*

This is reflected in crosscultural leadership shifts globally. Looking at African leaders, there are examples like Akinola Paul, a Nigerian who is pastor of Willesden Green Baptist Church in London; John Azumah, from northern Ghana, director of the Centre for Islamic Studies and Muslim-Christian Relations at the London School of Theology; Joshua Bogunjoko of Nigeria, SIM deputy international director for Europe and West Africa; Daniel K. Bourdanné from Chad, international general secretary of IFES in Oxford; and Tite Tiénou, senior vice president of education, dean and professor of theology of missions at Trinity Evangelical Divinity School. These are only a sprinkle of the changing nature of the church that calls for more crosscultural partnerships.

As I (Femi) reflect on this, I am reminded of Tony Campolo once describing the kingdom of God as a party. In many ways God has laid a bounteous table before us in the context of diverse cultures. Crosscultural missions partnership needs to recognize these cultures as part of God's mosaic, which points to the inexpressible diversity of a thousand tongues in harmonious worship before the Lamb on the throne on the last day.

I (Nikki) need to partner with church leaders in Latin America, because they know something about leading from the margins that is good for my soul. They know how to lead and influence from a position of powerlessness. And isn't that what the incarnation of Jesus is all about—coming and influencing us from a position of powerlessness, even though he had access to all power? Working with the church leaders in Latin America helps me understand an aspect of God that is outside of my American cultural mindset.

In a recent discussion with world leaders, in preparation for the Lausanne Congress, I (Nikki) was reminded of the gift that the Global South is to North American leaders. It was an unexpected picture of the gospel moving forward in an unexpected way.

Many Pilipinas work outside of their country. A significant portion of the Gross Domestic Product of the Philippines comes from remittances sent home from those working abroad. In many cities in Asia, the Middle East and even Europe, Sunday is the day when Pilipina domestics take the day off and gather together in parks and other public areas.

And with some of these women goes the gospel. Several agencies train domestics to carry the gospel with them. They don't have much power, but they have the presence of God traveling with them. They gossip the gospel in the kitchens with the women of a Saudi household. They say the future of Singapore is in the hands of the Pilipina. Why? Pilipina nannies are praying over the babies in their care. From a position of powerlessness, they speak the incarnational power of the gospel.[11]

There is something in this that resonates the very heart of God to me. Isn't this the way that Christ brought the gospel to us? He had every right to come from a position of power, and yet he came in the form of a powerless infant—so that we might know God. To me, the Pilipina women are not carrying out a strategy but responding to the very heart of God.

These examples show us that there are other ways to accomplish the purposes of God. Sometimes we, as Westerners, can be caught up in strategies and not notice the cultural assumptions that undergird them. The Pilipina domestics challenge our assumptions that when we cross cultural boundaries, we need to do so in a place of power. These women have different opportunities and therefore make different choices. It's this kind of thinking and approach that Westerners can learn through partnership. These pictures of incarnational ministry challenge our assumptions about what it means to walk alongside others. They challenge us to dismantle our models that rely on the power.

Who would have thought that domestic servants could reach elusive Middle Eastern households? Our Western mindset evaluates people by their economic worth. But Paul challenges us—members of one body—

to view others differently. He says that the seemingly weaker parts are essential (1 Corinthians 12:22). In the North American context, domestic servants are typically seen as a poor resource for reaching the world for Christ. But the Pilipinas reveal how indispensable they are.

In some ways, for those "at the top," partnership is critically important. It is a helpful check against the assumption that they are the best and that they are the originators of the mission. And global trends in the growth of the church show that North Americans may not be the dominant voice they once were. Partnership both transforms those involved and facilitates greater effectiveness. Partnership reveals our blind spots. We make mistakes and assumptions without partnership. In partnership we sharpen and strengthen each other. And ultimately partnership helps clarify our picture and understanding of "one body" life in God.

It is God's mission. And he placed each part in the body to play its role. Let's be people who are "one body" before we "do things" for people. What awaits is an invitation into a glorious, transformative experience in partnerships.

QUESTIONS FOR REFLECTION OR DISCUSSION

1. How have you experienced partnership? Can you give an example of a partnership done badly and one done well?

2. In what ways does the image of a body with many parts (1 Corinthians 12) help you understand what partnership should look like?

3. How do differences in power affect partnerships?

4. How is partnership being practiced within your movement or church?

5. How does the example of the Pilipina nannies suggest ways that Christians can better serve and minister?

6. What are one or two practices you or your group can work on in order to grow to be better partners?

→   →   →

RESOURCES

Borthwick, Paul. *Western Christians in Global Mission: What's the Role of the North American Church?* Downers Grove, Ill.: IVP Books, 2012.

Jenkins, Philip. *The Next Christendom: The Coming of Global Christianity.* New York: Oxford University Press, 2011.

Lederleitner, Mary T. *Cross-Cultural Partnerships: Navigating the Complexities of Money and Mission.* Downers Grove, Ill.: IVP Books, 2010.

Partnership. Compassion International's Ministry Philosophy Series, 2011. Available from Compassion International.

Round Trip. DVD and curriculum from *Christianity Today,* www.christianity today.com/help/media/pr_roundtrip.html.

NOTES

[1]Andrew Walls, "The Translation Principle in Christian History," in *Bible Translation and the Spread of the Church*, ed. Philip C. Stine (Boston: Brill, 1990), p. 38.

[2]Patrick Johnstone, *Operation World* (Carlisle, U.K.: OM Publishing, 1993), p. 25.

[3]David Barrett, ed., *World Christian Encyclopedia* (Nairobi: Oxford University Press, 1982), pp. 4, 9, 787.

[4]Andrew Walls, "Africa in Christian History-Retrospect and Prospect," *Journal of African Christian Thought* 1, no. 1 (June 1998): 2.

[5]See http://insight.typepad.co.uk/insight/2009/02/moon-landing-a-team-building-game.html.

[6]Meic Pearse, *Why the Rest Hates the West: Understanding the Roots of Global Rage* (Downers Grove, Ill.: InterVarsity Press, 2004), pp. 28-29.

[7]Ibid.

[8]Ibid., p. 16.

[9]Ibid., p. 17.

[10]Ibid.

[11]Lisa Espinelli Chinn contributed to this section. See also Miriam Adeney, *Kingdom Without Borders* (Downers Grove, Ill.: InterVarsity Press, 2009), pp. 27-28.

About Urbana

Since InterVarsity Christian Fellowship/USA and Inter-Varsity Canada's first Student Missions Conference in 1946, Urbana has influenced more than 250,000 people to devote their lives to God's global mission. Urbana's mission is to compel this generation to give their whole lives for God's global mission. Participants are challenged by missions leaders, are able to speak with hundreds of missions organizations, get to attend an amazing selection of seminars and tracks, and study the Bible inductively with other students listening for God's call on their lives. For more information, visit www.urbana.org.

Urbana Onward

God calls us to go into the world as his representatives. But we need not travel alone. Urbana Onward provides companions for the lifelong journey into missional living. This series offers concise resources for grappling with challenging issues. Trusted authors provide biblical and practical insights for following God's call in creative and courageous ways. Discover a bigger picture of God's global mission as he leads you onward.

Pursuing God's Call by Tom Lin, 978-0-8308-3459-4

Partnering with the Global Church by Nikki A. Toyama-Szeto and Femi B. Adeleye, 978-0-8308-3460-0

The Mission of Worship by Sandra Van Opstal, 978-0-8308-3462-4

Your Mind's Mission by Greg Jao, 978-0-8308-3461-7

Deepening the Soul for Justice by Bethany H. Hoang, 978-0-8308-3463-1

Spiritual Warfare in Mission by Mary Anne and Jack Voelkel, 978-0-8308-3464-8